Spirits of Various Kinds

By Helena P. Blavatsky

Copyright © 2021 Lamp of Trismegistus. All rights reserved. No part of this publication may be reproduced or transmitted in any form or by any means, electronic or mechanical, including photocopying, recording, or by any information storage and retrieval system, without permission in writing from Lamp of Trismegistus. Reviewers may quote brief passages.

ISBN: 978-1-63118-586-1

Esoteric Classics

Other Books in this Series and Related Titles

The Spirit of Zoroastrianism by Henry S Olcott (978–1–63118–564–9)

Clairvoyance and Psychic Abilities by A Besant &c (978-1-63118-403-1)

The Feminine Occult by various authors (978-1-63118-711-7)

Rosicrucian Rules, Secret Signs, Codes and Symbols by various (978-1-63118-488-8)

An Outline of Theosophy by C W Leadbeater (978-1-63118-452-9)

Paracelsus, the Four Elements and Their Spirits by M P Hall (978-1-63118-400-0)

Essays on Ancient Magic by Helena P Blavatsky (978-1-63118-535-9)

Essays on the Esoteric Tradition of Karma by A Besant &c (978-1-63118-426-0)

The Use of Evil by Annie Besant (978-1-63118-532-8)

Occult Arts by William Q. Judge (978-1-63118-559-5)

The Alchemical Catechism of Paracelsus by Paracelsus (978-1-63118-513-7)

Alchemy in the Nineteenth Century by Helena P Blavatsky (978-1-63118-446-8)

Qabbalistic Teachings and the Tree of Life by M P Hall (978-1-63118-482-6)

The Historic, Mythic and Mystic Christ by Annie Besant (978–1–63118–533–5)

The Hidden Mysteries of Christianity by Annie Besant (978–1–63118–534–2)

The Brotherhood of Religions by Annie Besant (978–1–63118–563–2)

Kali the Mother by Sister Nivedita (978-1-63118-558-8)

Arcane Formulas or Mental Alchemy by W W Atkinson (978-1-63118-459-8)

The Machinery of the Mind by Dion Fortune (978-1-63118-451-2)

Vision of the Spirit by C. Jinarajadasa (978-1-63118-560-1)

The Leadbeater Reader: A Selection of Occult Essays (978-1-63118-483-3)

Audio versions are also available on Audible, Amazon and Apple

Other Books in this Series and Related Titles

The Hidden Language of Symbolism by Annie Besant (978–1–63118–585–4)

Eastern Magic & Western Spiritualism by Henry S Olcott (978–1–63118–584–7)

Spiritual Progress and Practical Occultism by H P Blavatsky (978–1–63118–583–0)

Memory and Consciousness by Besant & Blavatsky (978–1–63118–582–3)

The Origin of Evil by Helena P Blavatsky (978–1–63118–581–6)

The Camp of Philosophy: Studies in Alchemy by Bloomfield (978–1–63118–580–9)

The Testaments of the Twelve Patriarchs (978–1–63118–579–3)

Occult or Exact Science? by Helena P Blavatsky (978–1–63118–578–6)

Occultism, Semi-Occultism & Pseudo Occultism by A Besant (978–1–63118–577–9)

The Fourth-Gospel and Synoptical Problem by G R S Mead (978–1–63118–576–2)

On the Bhagavad-Gita by T Subba Row &c (978–1–63118–575–5)

What Theosophy Does for Us by C W Leadbeater (978–1–63118–574–8)

Spiritual Life for Man by Annie Besant (978–1–63118–573–1)

The Mysteries by Annie Besant (978–1–63118–572–4)

Fundamental Ideas of Theosophy by Bhagwan Das (978–1–63118–571–7)

Dreams: What They Are and Caused by C W Leadbeater (978–1–63118–570–0)

Communication Between Different Worlds by Annie Besant (978–1–63118–569–4)

Animism, Magic and the Omnipotence of Thought by S Freud (978–1–63118–568–7)

Buddhism by F Otto Schrader (978–1–63118–567–0)

Death by W W Westcott (978–1–63118–566–3)

The Religion of Theosophy by Bhagwan Das (978–1–63118–565–6)

Audio versions are also available on Audible, Amazon and Apple

Table of Contents

Introduction...7

"Spirits" of Various Kinds...9

Chinese Spirits...29

Occultism is not the acquirement of powers, whether psychic or intellectual, though both are its servants. Neither is occultism the pursuit of happiness, as men understand the word; for the first step is sacrifice, the second, renunciation. Occultism is the science of life, the art of living.

INTRODUCTION

The word "esoteric" can be difficult to define. Esotericism in general can be seen less as a system of beliefs and more as a category, which encompasses numerous, different systems of beliefs. It's a bit of juxtaposition, since the word "esoteric" indicates something that few people know about, while the term itself broadly covers numerous philosophies, practices, areas of study and belief systems.

In a greater sense, Esotericism acts as a storehouse for secret knowledge, which is often considered ancient (by *tradition, if not by fact),* passed down from generation to generation, in private. At various times in history, simply possessing the knowledge of some of these subjects, was considered illegal and a jailable offence, if discovered. This usually included such general topics as Alchemy, Pharmacology, Qabalah, Hermeticism, Occultism, Ceremonial Magic, Astrology, Divination, Rosicrucianism and so on. Collectively, these areas of study were often referred to as the esoteric sciences.

Sometimes, the outer garment of a subject isn't esoteric, while what is hidden beneath it, is. As an example, Freemasonry isn't necessarily esoteric by nature (at *least not anymore),* but certain signs, passwords and handshakes given to the candidate during their initiation, are in fact, esoteric, in the sense that they are hidden from the general public.

Today, in the twenty-first century, such topics are readily available at bookstores across the country, and numerous mainsteam publishers offer beginners guides and coffee-table volumes on many of these subjects, intended for mass appeal. Books like *"The Secret"* have turned previously arcane topics into household knowledge. All that being the case, however, it isn't to say that there still aren't buried secrets to uncover, ancient wisdom being ignored and forgotten mysteries to be explored. In fact, it is often that we are only able to further our own studies by standing on the shoulders of these disappearing giants.

Lamp of Trismegistus is doing its part to help preserve humanity's esoteric history by making some of these classics available to those students who are seeking to unearth the knowledge of these ancient colossi.

So, be sure to check other titles from our *Esoteric Classics* series, as well as our *Occult Fiction, Theosophical Classics, Foundations of Freemasonry Series, Supernatural Fiction, Paranormal Research Series, Studies in Buddhism* and our *Christian Apocrypha Series*. You can also download the audio versions of most of these titles from Amazon, Apple or Audible, for learning on the go.

"SPIRITS" OF VARIOUS KINDS

Years have been devoted by the writer to the study of those invisible beings – conscious, semi- conscious, and entirely senseless – called by a number of names in every country under the sun, and known under the generic name of "spirits". The nomenclature applied to these denizens of spheres, good or bad, in the Roman Catholic Church alone, is endless. The Greek Kyriology of their symbolic names is a study. Open any account of creation in the first Purâna that comes to hand, and see the variety of appellations bestowed upon these divine and semi-divine creatures — the product of two kinds of creation (Mahattattva and Bhūta - the primary and the secondary), all evolved from the body of Brahma. The Urdhvasrota alone, [Urdhvasrota, the Gods so called because the bare sight of aliment stands to them in place of eating, "for there is satisfaction from the mere beholding of ambrosia," says a commentator on the Vishnu Purāna.] of the third creation, embrace a variety of beings with characteristics and idiosyncrasies sufficient for a life-study.

The same is true of the Egyptian, Chaldæan, Greek, Phœnician, or any other account. The hosts of these creatures are numberless. The old Pagans, however, and especially the Neo-Platonists of Alexandria, knew what they believed, and discriminated between the orders. None regarded them from such a sectarian standpoint as do the Christian Churches. They dealt with them far more wisely, on the contrary, as they made a better and a greater discrimination between the natures of these beings than did the Fathers of the Church, according to whose policy all the angels that were not recognized as the attendants upon the Jewish Jehovah were pronounced devils.

We find the effects of this belief, afterwards erected into a dogma, asserting themselves now in the Karma of the many millions of Spiritualists brought up and bred in the respective beliefs of their Churches. Though a Spiritualist may have divorced himself for many years from theological and clerical beliefs, though he be a liberal or an illiberal Christian, a deist or an atheist, having very wisely rejected belief in devils, and being too reasonable to regard his visitors as pure angels, he has taken up what he thinks a reasonable mean. He will acknowledge no other spirits than those of the dead.

This is his Karma, but it is also of the Churches collectively. In the latter such a stubborn fanaticism or *a parti pris* is only natural; it is their policy. In the free Spiritualist it is surely irrational. There cannot be two opinions upon this subject. It is not a question of either the belief in or the rejection of the existence of any "spirits".

If a man is a sceptic, an unbeliever, we have nothing to say. But when once he believes in the "spirits of the dead," the question changes. Where is that man or woman who, free from prejudice and preconceptions, can believe that in an infinite universe of life and being – let us say even in our solar system alone – in all this boundless space in which the Spiritualist locates his "Summer-Land," there are only two orders of conscious beings: men and their spirits; embodied mortals and disembodied immortals?

The future has in store for humanity strange surprises, and Theosophy – or rather its adherents – will be vindicated fully in no very distant ages. It is no use to re-argue a question that has been so fully discussed in *Isis Unveiled*, and that has brought only opprobrium, enmity, and persecution on the writer. Therefore we will not go out of our way to say much more. The elementals and the elementaries of the Kabalists and Theosophists have been sufficiently ridiculed, but, sadly enough, far too insufficiently dreaded. Nevertheless, from Porphyry and Iamblichus down to demonologists of the past centuries fact after fact has been given and proofs heaped upon proofs, but with little effect, as might be expected from the fairy tales told to Mr. Huxley in his nursery.

A queer book, that of the old Comte de Gabalis, immortalized by the Abbé de Villars, has been translated and published. Those who are humorously inclined are advised to read it and ponder over it. This advice is offered with the object of drawing a parallel. The writer read it several years ago, and has now read it again with more attention than formerly. Her humble opinion as regards the work is that one may search for months and never find the kind of demarcation between "spirits" of the séance-room and the sylphs and undines of the French satire. There is a sinister ring in the merry quips and jests of this writer who, while pointing the finger of ridicule at that in which he believed, had probably a presentiment of his own speedy Karma in the shape of assassination. [The work was published in Paris in 1670, and in 1675 the author was cruelly murdered on his way to Lyons from Languedoc, his native country.] The way he introduces the Comte de Gabalis is worthy of imitation – by unbelievers: " I was astonished One Remarkable day when I saw a man come in of the most exalted mien: who, saluting me gravely, said to me in the French Tongue, but in accent of a Foreigner: 'Adore my Son; adore the most glorious and great God of the Sages; and let not thyself be puft up with Pride, that he sends to thee one of the Children of Wisdom, to constitute thee a Fellow of their Society and make thee a partaker of the wonders of his Omnipotency.' " [*Sub-Mundanes, or the Elementaries of the Cabala*: "Being the history of spirits; reprinted from the text of the Abbé de Villars, Physio-Astro-Mystic, wherein it is asserted that there are in existence on earth rational creatures besides men" (Robert H. Fryar, Bath, 1886, p. 19]

There is only one answer to those who, taking advantage of such works, laugh at Occultism, "Servitissimo" gives it himself in his own chaffing way in his introductory "Letter to my Lord," in the above- named work.

"I would have persuaded him [the author] to have changed the whole frame of his work," he writes: "for this Drolling way of carrying it thus on does not to me seem proper to his Subject. These mysteries of the Cabal are serious Matters which many of my Friends do seriously study...the which are certainly most dangerous to jest with." (*Verbum satis est sapienti.*)

They are "dangerous," most undeniably. But since history began to record thoughts and facts, one-half of humanity has ever been sneering at the other half and ridiculing its most cherished beliefs. This, however, cannot change a fact into a fiction, nor can it destroy the sylphs, undines and gnomes, if there are any in Nature. For in league with salamanders the latter are more likely to destroy the unbelievers and damage insurance companies, notwithstanding that these believe still less in revengeful salamanders than in fires produced by accident and chance.

Theosophists believe in spirits no less than do Spiritualists, but to them they are as dissimilar in their variety as are the feathered tribes of the air. There are bloodthirsty hawks and vampire-bats among these, as there are doves and nightingales. They believe in angels, for many have seen them:

By the sick one's pillow,
Whose was the soft tone and the soundless tread?
Where smitten hearts were drooping like the willow,
They stood between the living and the dead.

But these were not the threefold materializations of the modern medium. And if our doctrines were all torn to pieces by the "drolleries: of a de Villars, that would not and could not interfere with the claim of the Occultists that their teachings are historical and scientific facts, whatever the garb in which they are presented to the profane. Since the first kings began reigning "by the grace of God," countless buffoons appointed to amuse majesties and highnesses have passed away; and most of these graceless individuals had more wisdom at the bottom of their humps and at their fingers' ends than all their royal masters put together had in their brainless pates. They alone had the inestimable privilege of speaking truths at the courts, and truths have always been laughed at.

This is a digression, but such works as that of the Comte de Gabalis have to be quietly explained and their true character shown, lest they should be made to serve as a sledge-hammer to pulverize those works which do not assume a humorous tone in speaking of mysterious, if not altogether sacred things, and which say what they have to say in direct language. And it is most positively maintained that there are more truths uttered in the witty railleries and gasconades of that satire — which is full of occult and actual facts — than most people, and Spiritualists specially, would care to learn. One single fact instanced and shown to exist now, at the present moment among the Spiritualists, will be sufficient to prove that we are right. It has often been said that white magic differs very little from the practices of sorcery except in its effects and results, good and bad motives being everything. The preliminary rules and conditions for entrance to Societies of Adepts are also identical in many points, both for those of the Right and the Left Path.

Thus Gabalis says to the author: "The Sages will never admit you into their Society if you do not renounce from this very present a Thing which cannot stand in competition with Wisdom. You must renounce all Carnal Commerce with women" (p. 27).

This is *sine qua non* with all would-be mystics – Rosicrucians or Yogis, Europeans or Asiatics; [We speak here of the well-known "ancient statutes" in the sorcery of the Asiatics and in the demonology of Europe. The witch had to renounce her husband; the wizard his marital rights over his legitimate human wife; as the Durga renounces to this day commerce with living women, as the New Orleans Voodoo does when employed in the "exercises of his powers." Every Kabalist knows this.] but it is also one with the Dugpas and Jadoos of Bhutan and India, as with the Voodoos and Nagals of New Orleans and Mexico – with an additional clause to it, however, in the statutes of the latter, and this is to have carnal commerce with male and female djiins, elementals or demons – call them by whatever names you please. [The Jewish Kabalist of Poland, when bent on revenge, calls a female spirit of Nergal to his help and to infuse into him power; the Musalman sorcerer calls a female djini; a Russian Kaldoon a deceased witch (vedyma); the Chinese malefactor has a female houen in his house at his command; the above intercourse is said to give magic powers and a supernal force.]

"I am making known nothing to you but the principles of the ancient Cabal," explains de Gabalis to his pupil. And he informs him that the elementals (whom he calls elementaries, the inhabitants of the four elements, namely, the sylphs, undines, salamanders and gnomes) live many ages, but that their souls are not immortal. (p. 29)

"In respect to Eternity ...they must finally resolve into nothing.... Our Fathers, the philosophers," goes on the *soi-disant* Rosicrucian, "speaking of God Face to Face, complained to him of the unhappiness of these People (the Elementals), and God, whose mercy is without bounds revealed to them that it was not impossible to find out a Remedy for this Evil. He inspired them that by the same means as man, by the alliance which he contracted with God, has been made Partaker of the Divinity, the Sylphs, the Gnomes, the Nymphs, and the Salamanders, by the alliance which they might contract with man, might be made partakers of Immortality. So a she-nymph, or a sylphide, becomes Immortal and capable of the Blessing to which we aspire, when they shall be so happy as to be married to a Sage; a Gnome or a Sylph ceases to be mortal from the moment that he Espouses one of our Daughters." (p. 31-32).

Having explained that this intercourse had led to the error in former ages of attributing the fall of the angels to their love of the women on earth (the gandharvas of the Hindus, if you please), when in fact it was simply "the desire which all these Elementary Inhabitants have of Allying themselves to men, as the only means to attain to the Immortality which they have not," — the "Sage" closes as follows: "No, no! our Sages have never erred so as to attribute the fall of the first Angels to their Love of Women, no more than they have put men under the Power of the Devil.....There was nothing criminal in all that. They were Sylphs which endeavored to become Immortal. Their innocent pursuits, far enough from being able to scandalize the Philosophers, have appeared so just to us that we are all resolved by common consent utterly to Renounce Women and entirely to give ourselves to Immortalizing of the Nymphs and Sylphs" (p. 33).

So with certain mediums, especially those of America, who boast of spiritual husbands and wives. We know personally several Spiritualists, men and women (and it is not those of Holland who will deny the fact) who escaped lunacy and death only by becoming Theosophists, and, by following our advice, got finally rid of their spiritual consorts of both sexes. Shall we be told again that this is calumny and invention? Then let those outsiders who are inclined to see naught but a holy, or at any rate an innocent pastime in the nightly and daily intercourse with the so-called "spirits of the dead," watch some of the developments of Spiritualism in the United States. Let those laugh who ridicule the beliefs of both Spiritualists and Theosophists - laughing at the warnings and explanations of the latter — let them, we say, explain after analyzing the matter dispassionately, the mystery and the rationale of such facts as the existence in the minds of certain mediums and sensitives of the conviction of their actual marriage with male and female spirits. Explanations of lunacy and hallucination will never do when placed face to face with the undeniable facts of spirit-materializations. There are "spirits" capable to drinking tea and wine, of eating apples and cakes, of kissing and touching the visitors at séance-rooms - all of which facts have been proved, as well as the existence of these visitors themselves - why should not those same spirits perform matrimonial duties as well?

But who are these spirits, and what is their nature? Shall we be told that the spirits, of Mme. De Sévigné or of a Delphine, two celebrated French authoresses, one of whom we abstain from naming out of regard to her surviving relatives, were the actual "spirits" of those two deceased ladies? That the latter felt a "spiritual affinity" for an idiotic, old, and slovenly Canadian medium, and thus became "his happy wife," as he boasts publicly, the result of the union being a number of "spiritual" children? And who is the astral husband of a well-known lady medium whom the writer knows personally? Let the reader get every information he can about this last development of "spiritual" intercourse. [The answer given (p. 133) by an alleged devil to S. Anthony, respecting the corporeity of the incubi and succubæ would do as well now, perhaps: "The Blessed S. Anthony" having inquired who he was, the little dwarf of the woods answered: "I am a mortal and one of the inhabitants of the Wilderness whom the gentile world under varied delusions worships under the names of Fauns, Satyrs, and Incubi," or "spirits of the dead," might have added this elemental, the vehicle of some elementary. This is a narrative of S. Hieronymus, who fully believed in it; and so do we, with certain amendments.] Let him think seriously over this, and then read Comte de Gabalis' work, especially the Appendix to it; and then he perchance, will be better able to appreciate the full gravity of the supposed chaff in the work in question, and to understand the value of the raillery in it. He will then see clearly the ghastly connection there is between fauns, satyrs, and incubi of S. Hieronymus, the sylphs and nymphs of the Comte de Gabalis, the "elementaries" of the Kabalists, and all these poetical spiritual "Lillies" of the "Harris Community," the astral "Napoleons" and the other departed Don Juans from the "Summer-Land," the "spiritual affinities from beyond the grave" of the modern world of mediums.

But all this still leaves open the question: Who are the spirits? For "where the doctors disagree" there must be room for doubt. And besides such ominous facts as that spirits are divided in their views upon reincarnation, just as Spiritualists and Spiritists are, "every man is not a proper champion for the truth not fit to take up the gauntlet in the cause of verity," says Sir T. Browne. An eminent man of science, Mr. W. Crookes, gave once a very wise definition of Truth, by showing how necessary it is to draw a distinction between truth and accuracy.

A person may be very truthful, he observed - that is to say, may be filled with the desire both to receive truth and to teach it, but unless that person have great natural powers of observation or have been trained by scientific study of some kind to observe, note, compare, and report accurately and in detail, he will not be able to give a trustworthy, accurate, and therefore true account of his experiences. His intentions may be honest, but if he have a spark of enthusiasm, he will be always apt to proceed to generalizations which may be both false and dangerous. In short, as another eminent man of science, Sir John Herschell puts it: "The grand - and indeed the only character - of truth is its capability of enduring the test of universal experience and coming unchanged out of every possible form of fair discussion."

Now the question is not what either the Spiritualists or Theosophists think personally of the nature of spirits and their degree of truthfulness; but what the "universal experience," demanded by Sir John Herschell says. Spiritualism is a philosophy (if it be one at all, which so far we deny) of but yesterday; Occultism and the philosophy of the East, whether absolutely or relatively, are teachings coming to us from an immense antiquity. And since both in the writings and traditions of the East, and in the numberless fragments and manuscripts left to us by the neo-Platonic Theosophists, as so on *ad infinitum*, we find the same identical testimony as to the extremely various and often dangerous nature of all these genii, demons, "gods," lares and "elementaries," now all confused into one heap under the name of "spirits," we cannot fail to recognize herein something "enduring the test of universal experience" and "coming unchanged out of every possible form" of observation and discussion.

Theosophists give only the product of an experience hoary with age; Spiritualists hold to their own views born some forty years ago, and based on their unflinching enthusiasm and emotionalism. But let any impartial, fair-minded witness to the doings of the "spirits" in America, one that is neither a Theosophist nor a Spiritualist, be asked: "What may be the difference between the vampire-bride from whom Apollonius of Tyana is said to have delivered a young friend of his, whom the nightly succuba was slowly killing, and the spirit-wives and husbands of our own day? Surely none, would be the correct answer. Those who do not shudder at this hideous revival of mediæval demonology and witchcraft may, at any rate, understand the reason why all of the numerous enemies of Theosophy none are so bitter and so implacable as some of the Spiritualists of the Protestant and of the Spiritists of Roman Catholic countries.

"Monstrum horrendum informe cui lumen ademptum" is the fittest epithet to be applied to most of the "Lillies" and "Joes" of the "Spirit-World." But we do not mean at all - following in this the example of one- sided Spiritualists who are determined to believe in no other "spirits" than those of the "dear-departed" ones - to maintain that, save nature-spirits or elementals, shells and "gods" and genii, there are no spirits from the invisible realms, or no really holy and grand spirits, who communicate with mortals. For that is not so. What the Occultists and Kabbalists have said all along, and what the Theosophists now repeat, is that holy Spirits will not visit promiscuous séance-rooms, nor will they intermarry with living men and women.

Belief in the existence of the invisible – but too often present – visitants from better and worse worlds than our own, is too deeply rooted in men's hearts to be torn out easily by the cold hand of either materialism or science. Charges of superstition, coupled with ridicule, have at best but served to breed additional hypocrisy and social cant among the better classes. For there are few men, if any, at the bottom of whose souls belief in superhuman and supersensuous creatures does not lie latent, to awaken into existence at the first opportunity. No need to repeat the long string of names of eminent and scientific converts to the phenomena of Spiritualism and to the creed itself, since for many years the catalogue has been published weekly by some spiritualistic papers. Many are the men of science who, having abandoned with their nursery-pinafores belief in kings of elves and fairy queens, and who would blush at being accused of believing in witchcraft, have fallen victims to the wiles of "Joes," "Daisies," and other spooks and "controls."

And once they have crossed the Rubicon they fear ridicule no longer. These scientists defend as desperately the reality of materialized and other spirits as if this were a mathematical law. Those soul aspirations that seem innate in human nature and that slumber only to awaken to intensified activity: those yearnings to cross the boundary of matter that make many a hardened sceptic turn into a rabid believer at the first appearance of that which to him is undeniable proof – all these complex psychological phenomena of human temperament – have our modern physiologists found the key to them? Will the verdict be ever *non compos mentis*, or "victim to fraud and psychology"? When we say with regard to unbelievers that they are "a handful," the statement is no under-valuation, for it is not those who shout the loudest against "degrading superstitions," - "the occult craze," and so on, who are the strongest in their scepticism. At the first opportunity they will be foremost among those who fall and surrender. And when one counts seriously the ever increasing millions of the Spiritualists, Occultists, and Mystics in Europe and America, one may well refuse to lament with Carrington over the "departure of the fairies." They are gone, says the poet:

> *They are flown —*
> *Beautiful fictions of our fathers, woven*
> *In superstition's web when time was young;*
> *And fondly loved and cherished — they are flown*
> *Before the wand of Science!*

We maintain that they have done nothing of the kind, and that on the contrary, it is these "fairies" — the beautiful far more than the hideous – who are seriously threatening under new masks and names to disarm science and break its "wand." Belief in "spirits" – legitimate because resting on the authority of experiment and observation – vindicates at the same time another belief, also regarded as a superstition, namely, polytheism. The latter is based upon a fact in Nature: spirits mistaken for Gods have been seen in every age by men: hence belief in many and various Gods. Monotheism, on the other hand, rests upon a pure abstraction. Whosoever saw God? – that God we mean, the Infinite and the Omnipotent, the one about whom monotheists talk so much? Polytheism – when once man claims the right of divine interference on his behalf – is logical and consistent with the philosophies of the East, all of which – whether pantheistic or deistic – proclaim the One to be an infinite Abstraction, an absolute Something, which utterly transcends the conception of the finite. Surely such a creed is more philosophical than the religion whose theology, proclaiming God in one place as a mysterious and an incomprehensible Being, shows him at the same time so human and so petty a god as to concern himself with the breeches of his chosen people, ["And thou shalt make them linen breeches to cover their nakedness, from the loins even unto the thighs they shall reach." – Exodus, xxviii, 42 – God a linen-draper and a tailor!] while neglecting to say anything definite about the immortality of their souls or their survival after death!

Thus belief in a host and hosts of spiritual Entities dwelling on various planes and higher spheres in the universe, in conscious intra-cosmic Beings, in fact, is logical and reasonable, while belief in an extra- cosmic God is an absurdity. And if Jehovah – who was so jealous about his Jews and commanded that they should have no other God save himself – was generous enough to bestow Moses upon Pharaoh as the Egyptian's monarch's deity, ["I have made thee a God to Pharaoh" Exodus, vii, 1]. why should not "Pagans" be allowed the choice of their own Gods? When once we believe in the existence and survival of our Egos, we may also believe in Dhyân Chohans. As Hare has it: "Man is a fixed being, made up of a spiritual and of a fleshly body; the Angels are pure spirits, herein nearer to God, only that they are created and finite in all respects, whereas God is infinite and uncreated." And if God is the latter, then God is not a "Being," but an incorporeal Principle not to be blasphemously anthropomorphized. The Angels, or the Dhyân Chohans, are the "Living Ones;" that Principle, the "Self-Existent," the eternal, and all-pervading Cause of all causes, is only the abstract noumenon of the "River of Life," whose ever-rolling waves create angels and men alike, the former being simply "men of a superior kind," as Young thought.

The masses of mankind are thus well justified in believing in a plurality of Gods; nor is it by calling them spirits, angels, and demons that Christians are less polytheistic than are their Pagan brethren. The twenty or thirty millions of the now-existing

Spiritualists and Spiritists minister to their dead as jealously as the modern Chinaman and the Hindus minister to their Houen, [The Houen in China is "the second soul," or human vitality, the principle which animates the ghost," as explained by the missionaries from China – simply the astral. The Houen, however, is as distinct from the "Ancestors" as the Bhūts are from the Pitrs in India.] Bhûts and Pishâchas; the Pagans, however, only keep them quiet from post-mortem mischief. On the other hand, we have demonstrated fully in the Proem to the *Secret Doctrine* that the worship of angels and spirits by the Roman Catholics and the Christians of the Oriental Churches, representing several hundred millions of men, women and children, who worship armies of Saints besides – is idolatrous as any idol-worship in India and China. The only difference one can see is that the Pagans are sincere in calling their religion polytheism, whereas the Churches – in company with the Protestant Spiritualists, whether consciously or otherwise – put a mask on theirs by claiming for it the title of a monotheistic Church.

There is a philosophy in dealing with the question of spirits in Indian "idolatry" that is conspicuously absent from the western definitions of them. The Devas are, so to say, the embodied powers of states of matter, more refined than those with which we are familiar. [See *Secret Doctrine*, Appendix, II, book ii: "Gods, Monads and Atoms."] In the Vedas the gods are mentioned as being eleven in number, where each one of the eleven stands as the representative of the class to which he belongs. Each of these classes again is subdivided into three, thus yielding the thirty-three classes of primary Gods, common alike to the Hindu and Buddhistic systems, [See Chinese, Burmese, and Siamese Mythologies.]as may be seen on reference to Beale's *Catena of Chinese Buddhism*. Each one of these thirty-three, subdivided again, admits further, division almost indefinitely like the substantial monads of Liebnitz; a fact which is expressed by the number of the Gods being given as thirty-three crores (33x10,000,000)

The key to the esoteric significance of these Gods would enable modern physical science, and chemistry especially, to achieve a progress that they may not otherwise reach in a thousand years to come, as every God has a direct connection with, and a representative in, its bodily fabric, so to say, in invisible atoms and visible molecules – physical and chemical particles. (See again "Gods, Monads, and Atoms.")

Although these Gods are said to be "superior to men in some respects," it must not be concluded that the latent potencies of the human Spirit are at all inferior to those of the devas. Their faculties are more expanded than those of ordinary man, but the conclusion of their evolution prescribes a limit to their expansion to which the human Spirit is not subjected. This fact has been well symbolized in the *Mahâbhârata* by the single-handed victory of Arjuna, under the name of Nara (man) over the whole host of Devas and Devayonis (the lower elementals). And we find reference to the same power in man in the *Bible*, for St. Paul distinctly says to his audience" "Know ye not that we shall judge angels?" (1 Cor., v, 8), and speaks of the astral body of man *(the soma psychikon)* and the spiritual body *(soma pneumatikon)*, which "hath not flesh and bones," but has still an ethereal form. An Adept, by putting himself under a special course of training and initiation may attain the status of a Deva but by such a course he is debarred from further progress along the true path (See "The Elixir of Life" in *Five Years of Theosophy*). The story of Nahusa gives a glimpse of the truth as known to the Initiates.

A description of the order of beings called Devas – whose variety is so great that it could not be attempted here – is given in some occult treatises. There are high Devas and lower ones, higher elementals and those far below man and even animals. But all these have been or will be men, the former will again be reborn on higher planets and in other Manvantaras. One thing may however be mentioned. The pitrs (or our "lunar ancestors"), and the communication of mortals with them, are several times mentioned by Spiritualists as an argument that Hindus do believe in, and even worship, "spirits." This is a great mistake. It is not the Pitrs individually that were ever consulted, but their stored wisdom collectively, that wisdom being shown mystically and allegorically on the bright side of the moon. A few words may perhaps serve as valuable hints to Occultists and students.

What the Brâhmanas invoke are not the "spirits" of the departed ancestors, the full significance of which name is shown in the *Secret Doctrine*, where the genesis of man is given. The most highly-developed human spirit will always declare, while leaving its tenement of clay: "*Nacha punarâvartate*" ("I am not coming back"), and is thus placed beyond the reach of any living man. But to comprehend fully the nature of the "lunar ancestors," and their connection with the "moon" would necessitate the revelation of occult secrets which are not intended for public hearing. Therefore no more can be given out beyond what is said here. One of the names of the moon is "Soma" in Samskrt, and this is also the name, as is well known, of the mystic drink of the Brâhmanas, showing the connection between the two. A "Soma-drinker" attains the power of placing himself in direct *rapport* with the bright side of the moon, and of thus deriving inspiration from the concentrated intellectual energy of the blessed ancestors. This concentration of energy – and the fact of the moon being a storehouse of that energy – is the secret, the meaning of which must not be revealed, beyond the mere fact that it is continuously pouring upon the earth from the bright side of the orb.

This pours out in one stream (for the ignorant), but it is really of a dual nature; one giving life and wisdom, the other being lethal. He who can separate the former from the latter —as Kalahamsa separated milk from the water which was mixed with it, and thus showed great wisdom – will have his reward. The word "Pitṛ" does mean, no doubt, the "ancestor," but that which is invoked is the "lunar wisdom," as Manu calls it, not the "lunar ancestor." It is this wisdom that is invoked by Qu-ta-my, the Chaldæan, in the *Nabathæan Agriculture*, he who wrote down "the revelation of the moon." But there is the other side to this. If most of the Brâhmanical religious ceremonies are connected with the full moon, the dark ceremonials of the sorcerers take place at the new moon and at its last quarter. For similarly, when the lost human being, or sorcerer, attains the consummation of his depraved career, all the evil inspiration comes down upon him as a dark incubus of iniquity from the "dark side of the moon" – which is a *terra incognita* to science, but is a well explored land to the Adept. The sorcerer, the Dugpa, who always performs his hellish rites on the day of the new moon – when the benignant influence of the Pitrs is at its lowest ebb – crystallizes some of the satanic energy of his predecessors in evil, and turns it into his own vile uses; while the Brâhmana on the other hand, pursues a corresponding but benevolent course with the energy bequeathed to him by the Pitrs.

This is the true Spiritualism, of which the heart and soul have been entirely missed by the modern Spiritualists. When the day of the full revelation comes it will be seen that the so-called "superstitions" of Brahmanism, and of the ancient Pagans in general, were merely natural and physical sciences, veiled from the profane eyes of the ignorant multitudes, for fear of desecration and abuse, by allegorical and symbolical disguises that modern science has failed to penetrate.

It follows from the foregoing that no Theosophist, whether Gentile or Christian, deist or pantheist, has ever believed in or helped to spread "degrading superstitions" any more than has any other philosophical or scientific society. If some Theosophists – most of them indeed – openly confess their belief in Dhyân Chohans (disembodied men from other preceding Manvantaras), in Pitrs (our real, genuine ancestors), and in the hosts of their spirits – mundane, sub-mundane, and supra-mundane– they do no worse than the whole Christian world did, does, and will do. In this they are far more honorable than those who hide that belief and keep it *sub rosa*. The only difference between spirits of other societies, sects and bodies, and ours lies in their names and in dogmatic assertions with regard to their natures. In those whom the millions of Spiritualists call the "spirits of the dead," and in whom the Roman Church sees the devils of the host of Satan, we see neither. We call them Dhyân Chohans, Devas, Pitrs, Elementals, high and low, and know them as the "Gods" of the Gentiles – imperfect at times, never wholly so. Each order has its name, its place, its functions assigned to it in Nature, and each host is the complement and crown of his own globes; hence all are a natural and logical necessity in Kosmos.

CHINESE SPIRITS

The following notes have been collected partly from an old work by a French missionary who lived in China for over forty years; some from a very curious unpublished work by an American gentleman who has kindly lent the writer his notes; some from information given by the Abbé Huc to the Chevalier Des Mousseaux and the Marquis De Mirville—for these the last two gentlemen are responsible. Most of our facts, however, come from a Chinese gentleman residing for some years in Europe.

Man, according to the Chinaman, is composed of four root-substances and three acquired "semblances." This is the magical and universal occult tradition, dating from an antiquity which has its origin in the night of time. A Latin poet shows the same source of information in his country, when declaring that:—

> Bis duo sunt hominis: manes, caro, spiritus, umbra;
> Quatuor ista loca bis duo suscipiunt.
> Terra tegit carnem, tumulum circumvolat umbra,
> Orcus habet manes, spiritus astra petit.

The phantom known and described in the Celestial Empire is quite orthodox according to occult teachings, though there exist several theories in China upon it.

The *human* soul, says the chief (temple) teaching, helps man to become a rational and intelligent creature, but it is neither simple (homogeneous) nor spiritual; it is a compound of all that is subtle in matter. This "soul" is divided by its nature and actions into two principal parts: the LING and the HOUEN. The *ling* is the better adapted of the two for spiritual and intellectual operations, and has an "upper" *ling* or soul over it which is divine. Moreover, out of the union of the lower *ling* and *houen* is formed, during man's life, a third and mixed being, fit for both intellectual and physical processes, for good and evil, while the *houen* is absolutely bad. Thus we have four principles in these two "substances," which correspond, as is evident, to our Buddhi, the divine "upper" *ling;* to Manas, the lower *ling,* whose twin, the *houen,* stands for Kama-rupa—the body of passion, desire and evil; and then we have in the "mixed being" the outcome or progeny of both *ling* and *houen*—the "Mayavi," the astral body.

Then comes the definition of the third root-substance. This is attached to the body only during life, the body being the fourth substance, pure matter; and after the death of the latter, separating itself from the corpse—but not before its complete dissolution—it vanishes in thin air like a shadow with the last particle of the substance that generated it. This is of course Prâna, the life-principle or vital form. Now, when man dies, the following takes place:—the "upper" *ling* ascends heavenward—into Nirvâna, the paradise of Amitâbha, or any other region of bliss that agrees with the respective sect of each Chinaman—carried off by the *Spirit of the Dragon of Wisdom* (the seventh principle); the body and *its* principle vanish gradually and are annihilated; remain the *ling-houen* and the "mixed being." If the man was good, the "mixed being" disappears also after a time; if he was bad and was entirely under the sway of *houen*, the absolutely evil principle, then the latter transforms his "mixed being" into *koueïs*—which answers to the Catholic idea of a damned soul¹—and, imparting to it a terrible vitality and power, the *kouëis* becomes the *alter ego* and the executioner of *houen* in all his wicked deeds. The *houen* and *kouëis* unite into one shadowy but strong entity, and may, by separating at will, and acting in two different places at a time, do terrible mischief.

The *kouëis* is an *anima damnata* according to the good missionaries, who thus make of the milliards of deceased "unbaptized" Chinamen an army of devils, who, considering they are of a material substance, ought by this time to occupy the space between our earth and the moon and feel themselves as much at ease as closely packed-up herrings in a tin-box.

"The *kouëis*, being naturally wicked," says the Memoire, "do all the evil they can. They hold the middle between man and the brute and participate of the faculties of both. They have all the vices of man and every dangerous instinct of the animal. Sentenced to ascend no higher than our atmosphere, they congregate around the tombs and in the vicinity of mines, swamps, sinks and slaughter-houses, everywhere wherein rottenness and decay are found. The emanations of the latter are their favourite food, and it is with the help of those elements and atoms, and of the vapours from corpses, that they form for themselves *visible and fantastic bodies* to deceive and frighten men with. . . . These miserable spirits with deceptive bodies seek incessantly the means for preventing men from getting salvation" (read, being baptized), ". . . and of forcing them to become damned as they themselves are." (p. 222, *Memoires concernant l'histoire, les*

---

¹ The spiritual portion of the *ling* becomes *chen* (divine and saintly), after death, to become *hien*—an absolute saint (a Nirvanee when joined entirely with the "Dragon of Wisdom").

sciences, les arts, les mœurs, etc., des Chinois, par les Missionaires de Pekin, 1791).[2]

This is how our old friend, the Abbé Huc, the Lazarist, unfrocked for showing the origin of certain Roman Catholic rites in Tibet and China, describes the *houen.*

"What is the *houen* is a question to which it is difficult to give a clear answer. . . . It is, if you so like it, something vague, something between *a spirit, a genii, and vitality.*" (see Huc's *Voyage à la Chine,* vol. II, p. 394).

He seems to regard the *houen* as the future operator in the business of resurrection, which it will effect by attracting to itself the atomic substance of the body, which will be thus re-formed on the day of resurrection. This answers well enough the Christian idea of one body and merely one personality to be resurrected. But if the *houen* has to unite on that day the atoms of all the bodies the Monad had passed through and inhabited, then even that "very

---

[2] According to the most ancient doctrines of magic, violent deaths and leaving the body exposed, instead of burning or burying it—led to the discomfort and pain of its *astral* (Linga Sarira), which died out only at the dissolution of the last particle of the matter that had composed the body. Sorcery or black magic, it is said, had always availed itself of this knowledge for necromantic and sinful purposes, "Sorcerers offer to unrestful souls decayed remnants of animals to force them to appear" (see Porphyry, *Sacrifice*). St. Athanasius was accused of the black art, for having preserved the hand of Bishop Arsenius for magical operations. "Patet quod animæ illæ quæ, post mortem, adhuc, relicta corpora diligunt, quemadmodum animæ sepultura carentiumt et adhuc in turbido illo humidoque spiritu [the spiritual or fluidic body, the *houen*] circa cadavera sua oberrant, tanquam circa cognatum aliquod eos alliciens," etc. See Cornelius Agrippa *De Occulta Philosophia,* pp. 354-5; *Le Fantôme Humain* by Des Mousseaux. Homer and Horace have described many a time such evocations. In India it is practised to this day by some *Tântrikas.* Thus modern sorcery, as well as white magic, occultism and spiritualism, with their branches of mesmerism, hypnotism, etc., show their doctrines and methods linked to those of the highest antiquity, since the same ideas, beliefs and practices are found now as in old Aryavarta, Egypt and China, Greece and Rome. Read the treatise, careful and truthful as to facts, however erroneous as to the author's conclusions, by P. Thyrée, *Loca Infesta,* and you will find that the localities most favourable for the evocations of spirits are those where a murder has been committed, a burying ground, deserted places, etc.

cunning creature" might find itself not quite equal to the occasion. However, as while the *ling* is plunged in felicity, its *ex-houen* is left behind to wander and suffer, it is evident that the *houen* and the "elementary" are identical. As it is also undeniable that had disembodied man the faculty of being at one and the same time in Devachan and in Kama-loka, whence he might come to us, and put in an occasional appearance in a séance-room or elsewhere—then man—as just shown by the *ling* or *houen*—would be possessed of the double faculty of experiencing a *simultaneous and distinct feeling* of two contraries—*bliss and torture*. The ancients understood so well the absurdity of this theory, knowing that no absolute bliss could have place wherein there was the smallest alloy of misery, that while supposing the higher Ego of Homer to be in *Elysium*, they showed the Homer weeping by the Acherusia as no better than the *simulacrum* of the poet, his empty and deceptive image, or what we call the "shell of the false personality."[3]

There is but *one* real Ego in each man and it must necessarily be either in one place or in another, in bliss or in grief.[4]

The *houen*, to return to it, is said to be the terror of men; in China, "that horrid spectre" troubles the living, *penetrates* into houses

---

[3] See Lucretius *De Nat. Rerum* I., 1, who calls it a *simulacrum*.

[4] Though antiquity (like esoteric philosophy) seems to divide soul into the divine and the animal, *anima divina* and *anima bruta*, the former being called *nous* and *phren*, yet the two were but the double aspect of a unity. Diogenes Laërtius (*De Vit. Clar. Virc.* I., 8, 30) gives the common belief that the animal soul, *phren*—φρήν, generally the diaphragm—resided in the stomach, Diogenes calling the *anima bruta* θύμος. Pythagoras and Plato also make the same division, calling the divine or rational soul λόγον and the irrational ἄλογον. Empedocles gives to men and animals a dual soul, not two souls as is believed. The Theosophists and Occultists divide man into seven principles and speak of a divine and animal soul: but they add that Spirit being one and indivisible, all these "souls" and principles are only its aspects. Spirit alone is immortal, infinite, and the one reality—the rest is all evanescent and temporary, illusion and delusion. Des Mousseaux is very wroth with the late Baron Dupotet, who places an intelligent "spirit" in each of our organs, simply because he is unable to grasp the Baron's idea.

and closed objects, and *takes possession* of people, as "spirits" are shown to do in Europe and America—the *houens* of children being of still greater malice than the *houens* of adults. This belief is so strong in China that when they want to get rid of a child they carry it far away from home, hoping thereby to puzzle the *houen* and make him lose his way home.

As the *houen* is the fluidic or gaseous likeness of its defunct body, in judicial medicine experts use this likeness in cases of suspected murders to get at the truth. The formulæ used to evoke the *houen* of a person dying under suspicious circumstances are officially accepted and these means are resorted to very often, according to Huc, who told Des Mousseaux (see *Les Mediateurs de la Magie*, p. 310) that the instructing magistrate after having recited the evocation over the corpse, used vinegar mixed with some mysterious ingredients, as might any other necromancer. When the *houen* has appeared, it is always in the likeness of the victim *as it was* at the moment of its death. If the body has been *burned* before judicial enquiry, the *houen* reproduces on its body the wounds or lesions received by the murdered man—the crime is proven and justice takes note of it. The sacred books of the temples contain the complete formulas of such evocations, and even the name of the murderer may be forced from the complacent *houen*. In this the Chinamen were followed by Christian nations however. During the Middle Ages the suspected murderer was placed by the judges before the victim, and if at that moment blood began to flow from the open wounds, it was held as a sign that the accused was the criminal. This belief survives to this day in France, Germany, Russia, and all the Slavonian countries. "The wounds of a murdered man will re-open at the approach of his murderer" says a jurisprudential work (Binsfeld, *De Conf. Malef.*, p. 136).

> "The *houen* can neither be buried underground nor drowned; he travels *above* the ground and prefers keeping at home."

In the province of Ho-nan the teaching varies. Delaplace, a bishop in China[5] tells of the "heathen Chinee" most extraordinary stories with regard to this subject.

> "Every man, they say, has three *houens* in him. At death one of the *houens* incarnates in a body he selects for himself; the other remains in, and with, the family, and becomes the *lar;* and the third watches the tomb of its corpse. Papers and incense are burnt in honour of the latter, as a sacrifice to the *manes;* the domestic *houen* takes his abode in the family record-tablets amidst engraved characters, and sacrifice is also offered to him, *hiangs* (sticks made of incense) are burnt in his honour, and funeral repasts are prepared for him; in which case the two *houens* will keep quiet"—if *they are those of adults, nota bene.*

Then follows a series of ghastly stories. If we read the whole literature of magic from Homer down to Dupotet we shall find everywhere the same assertion: Man is a *triple*, and esoterically a *septenary*, compound of mind, of reason, and of an eidolon, and these three are (during life) one.

> "I call the soul's idol that power which vivifies and governs the body, whence are derived the senses, and through which the soul displays the strength of the senses and FEEDS A BODY WITHIN ANOTHER BODY." (*Magie Dévoilée*, Dupotet, p. 250).

---

[5] *Annales de la propagation de la foi.* No.143; July, 1852.

"Triplex unicuique homini dæmon, bonus est proprius custos," said Cornelius Agrippa, from whom Dupotet had the idea about the "soul's *idol.*" For Cornelius says:

"Anima humana constat mente, ratione et *idolo.* Mens illuminat rationem; ratio fluit in idolum; idolum autem animæ est supra naturam quæ *corporis et animæ* quodam modo *nodus est.* Dico autem animæ idolum, *potentiam* illam VIVICATIVAM *et rectricem corporis* sensuum originem, per quam . . . alit in corpore corpus" (*De Occulta Philos.*, pp. 357, 358).

This is the *houen* of China, once we divest him of the excrescence of popular superstition and fancy. Nevertheless the remark of a Brahman made in the review of "A Fallen Idol" (*Theosophist*, Sept., 1886, p. 793)—whether meant seriously or otherwise by the writer—that "if the rules [or mathematical proportions and measurements] are not accurately followed in every detail, an *idol* is liable to be taken possession of by some powerful evil spirit"—is quite true. And as a moral law of nature—a counterpart to the mathematical—if the rules of harmony in the world of causes and effects are not observed during life, then our *inner* idol is as liable to turn out a maleficent demon (a *bhoot*) and to be taken possession of by other "evil" spirits, which are called by us "Elementaries" though treated almost as gods by sentimental ignoramuses.

Between these and those who, like Des Mousseaux and De Mirville, write volumes—a whole library!—to prove that with the exception of a few Biblical apparitions and those that have favoured Christian saints and good Catholics, there never was a phantom, ghost, spirit, or "god," that had appeared that was not a *ferouer*, an *impostor*, a *usurpator*—Satan, in short, in one of his masquerades—there is a long way and a wide margin for him who would study Occult laws and Esoteric philosophy. "A *god* who eats and drinks and receives sacrifice and honour can be but an evil spirit" argues De Mirville. "The bodies of the evil spirits who were angels have deteriorated by their *fall* and partake of the qualities of a more condensed air" [ether?], teaches Des Mousseaux (*Le Monde magique*, p. 287). "And this is the reason of their appetite when they devour the funeral repasts the Chinese serve before them to propitiate them; they are demons."

Well, if we go back to the supposed origin of Judaism and the Israelite nation, we find *angels* of light doing just the same—if "good appetite" be a sign of Satanic nature. And it is the same Des Mousseaux who, unconsciously, lays, for himself and his religion, a trap.

"See," he exclaims, "the angels of God descend under the green trees near Abraham's tent. They eat *with appetite* the bread and meat, the butter and the milk prepared for them by the patriarch." (*Gen.* xviii, 2, *et seq*).

Abraham dressed a whole "calf tender and good" and "they did eat" (v. 7 and 8); and baked cakes and milk and butter besides. Was their "appetite" any more *divine* than that of a "John King" drinking tea with rum and eating toast in the room of an English medium, or than the appetite of a Chinese *houen?*

The Church has the power of discernment, we are assured; she knows the difference between the three, and judges by their bodies. Let us see. "These [the Biblical] are real, genuine spirits"!

Angels, beyond any doubt (*certes*), argues Des Mousseaux. "Theirs are bodies which, no doubt, in dilating could, in virtue of the extreme tenuity of the substance, become transparent, then melt away, dissolve, lose their colour, become less and less visible, and finally disappear from our sight" (p. 388).

So can a "John King" we are assured, and a Pekin *houen* no doubt. Who or what then can teach us the difference if we fail to study the uninterrupted evidence of the classics and the Theurgists, and neglect the Occult sciences?

www.ingramcontent.com/pod-product-compliance
Lightning Source LLC
LaVergne TN
LVHW041503070426
835507LV00009B/778